Starting *Art*

BOOK 1

Mary Carroll ◆ Katie Long

THE O'BRIEN PRESS

PINE FOREST ART

This edition published 1999 by The O'Brien Press Ltd.
20 Victoria Road, Dublin 6, Ireland.
Tel. +353 1 4923333; Fax. +353 1 4922777
e-mail: books@obrien.ie
website: http://www.obrien.ie
Co-published with Pine Forest Art Centre

Originally published 1996 by Pine Forest Art Centre

ISBN: 0-86278-607-X

British Library Cataloguing-in-publication Data
Carroll, Mary, 1954 -
Starting art : art activities with children. - 2nd ed.
1.Art - Juvenile literature 2.Handicraft - Juvenile literature
I.Title II.Long, Katie III.Pine Forest starting art
745

1 2 3 4 5 6 7 8 9 10
99 00 01 02 03 04 05 06 07

Cover and prelims layout and design: The O'Brien Press Ltd.
Photographs, pages 5 and 46: Robert Vance
All other photographs: Dennis Mortell
Printing: Zure, Spain

CONTENTS

PINE FOREST ART CENTRE is a unique art education centre catering for children and young adults. The centre is situated in Glencullen, high in the Dublin Mountains, surrounded by fields, woods and streams. Its uniqueness derives both from its beautiful location and from the philosophy of teachers Mary Carroll and Katie Long. Assisted by Katie since 1987, Mary has devoted the past twenty-five years to designing and teaching art activity programmes. This book is a culmination of that work, providing a wide range of projects, with defined objectives, that have been tried and tested by the many children who have attended courses at the centre over that time.

The philosophy of the Art Centre is that a happy and successful experience in creating and exploring art can awaken and stimulate a lifelong appreciation of, and participation in, creative activity. To this end, Mary Carroll and Katie Long guide the children through a wide range of activities, depending on their age-group, helping them to explore their artistic abilities. These activities are coupled with an emphasis on appreciation and understanding of the natural environment. The children are taken on nature trails for out-of-doors sketching and to collect natural materials for their projects. As well as courses for fun, the centre also runs portfolio courses for young adults who are preparing to enter third-level education.

Pine Forest Art Books allow children everywhere to share in this wonderful experience.

NOW AVAILABLE
Starting Art 1 (ages 4-8)
Discovering Art 1 (ages 8-12)
To be followed later by *Discovering Art 2* and *Starting Art 2*. These four books provide a comprehensive art course for children, teachers and parents.

AND FOR CHILDREN

Art Explorer Books 1 and *2*
32 page books in full colour covering eight art subjects each. These books can be used by the child without adult help – at home, in school or on holidays.

Pine Forest Art Centre, Glencullen, Co. Dublin, Ireland. Tel: 01 2955598/2941220 Fax: 01 2941221

STARTING ART is a practical handbook aimed at teachers and parents of 4-8 year olds who want to introduce their pupils/children to basic art skills. The book is structured to allow an adult facilitator to guide the child through the various activities – children of this age need help to interpret instructions and to handle the requisite equipment. It also allows adult and child to work together in a way that is mutually beneficial.

The book is divided into various activities covering a wide range of art techniques, for example, painting, finger puppets, candle-making and hand printing. Each project is accompanied by step-by-step instructions and advice on materials. The variety of things to do provides a sound skill basis and stimulates the child's interest in experimenting with different media.

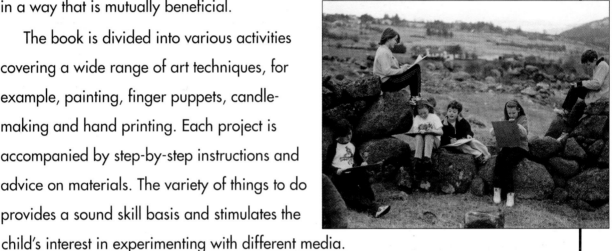

There are notes at the end of the book explaining the objective of each activity; this allows the parent or teacher to gradually introduce the concepts behind the projects, for example, colour theory, design, manipulation of materials and composition. The aim of this method is to debunk the myth that artistic ability is an exclusive gift and to encourage each child to express him/herself freely and confidently. Because these concepts are introduced as part of the activity the child is free to learn in an enjoyable, unforced way, ensuring that art, both as activity and appreciation, remains an imaginative delight in individual expression.

Rainbows

Theme

A Rainbow

When you paint a rainbow you use the three Primary Colours red, yellow and blue.

When you mix two of the Primary Colours together Fig 1, you make a Secondary Colour, green, purple or orange Fig 2.

Red + Yellow = Orange
Yellow + Blue = Green
Blue + Red = Purple Fig 3

Materials

Paper	white cartridge
Paint	yellow, red, blue and black
	or
Pastels	**or**
Crayons	the sort that can be blended when wet
Water	to wash brushes

Equipment

Paint Brushes

Tubs	for paint and water
Kitchen roll	(tissue)
Newspaper	

Fig 1 Primary Colours

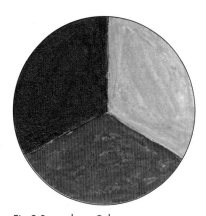

Fig 2 Secondary Colours

Preparation

Cover the table with newspaper. Organise the paints so that you have easy access to each colour and to water to wash your brush.

Starting Point

Start with a yellow semicircle to represent the sun shining through the raindrops to make a rainbow.

Trouble Shooter

Apply the paint thickly.
Use as little water as possible.
After washing your brush be sure to dry off any excess water from it.
Make the yellow band of colour much wider than the red, and the red wider than the blue.
This is because darker colours are stronger than lighter colours so you need more of the lighter colour.

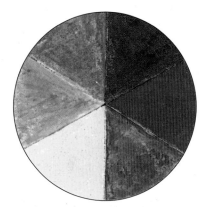

Fig 3 Primary and Secondary Colours

Method

1 Paint a yellow semicircle at the base of the page.

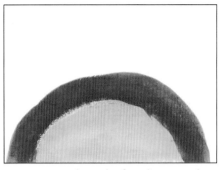

2 Paint a band of red around it.

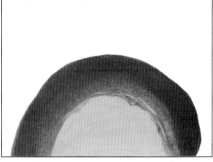

3 With a damp brush blend the red into the yellow around the edges to make a band of orange.

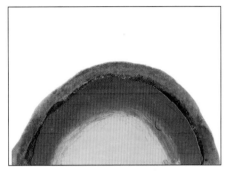

4 Paint a band of blue around the red.

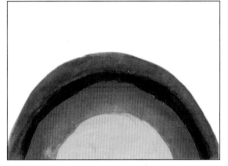

5 Blend the red into the blue to make purple.

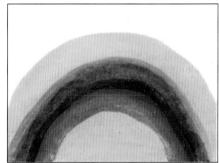

6 Paint another wide band of yellow around the blue and blend the blue into it to make green.

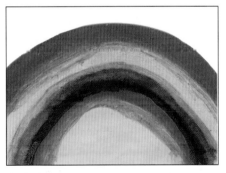

7 Paint another band of red.

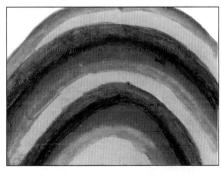

8 Blend it into the yellow and continue as before until you have filled the page.

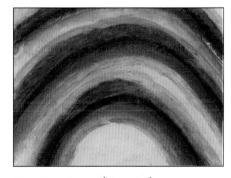

9 Continue the rainbow colours out to the corners of the page.

VARIATIONS

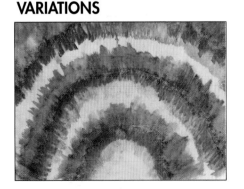

AN EXPLODING RAINBOW

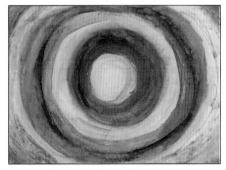

A RAINBOW IN SPACE

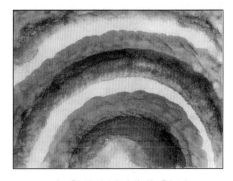

A CURLY RAINBOW

Things We Eat

Theme
Food

Starting Point
Think about a plate of food. Decide what food you would like to make to put on your plate.

Materials
Modelling Material air drying
Paper plate
Felt tip pens to decorate plate
Powder Paint
    and
PVA glue to mix in if you are pre-colouring a monochrome material
Acrylic Paint if you are using a monochrome material and are applying colour after you have made the model

Equipment
Modelling tools
    or
Tools improvised from skewers and lollypop sticks
Plastic to cover tables

Preparation
Cover the tables with plastic. If the modelling material you are using is monochrome, that is all one colour, it is more effective to mix the paint and PVA glue with it before using it. Allow varying amounts of the different colours depending on what food you are going to make.

Method
Only take enough modelling material on to your board to make one piece of food at a time.

Follow the step-by-step method for the ones you want to make and add other items that you think of yourself.

When you have all the pieces you want made, decorate the cardboard plate with felt tip pens Fig1. When the food is dry, arrange it on the plate.

Trouble Shooter
Whether you are painting with acrylic paints or using coloured material make sure the food is thoroughly dried out before arranging it on a plate, otherwise the pieces may stick to each other.

Method

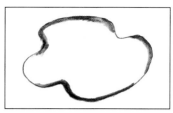

1 Make a small ball of white. Flatten it and push in the edges to make it irregular. You could also put a little bit of brown at the edges.

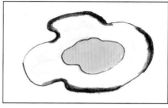

2 Make a small ball of yellow and press it into the centre.

Egg

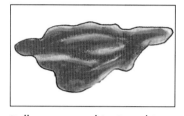

1 Make a piece of pink into a roll, flatten it and push it into the shape of a piece of bacon.

2 Roll out some white into thin strips and add some white streaks to the bacon.

Bacon

1 Make a ball of red.

2 Divide it in half and add yellow seeds.

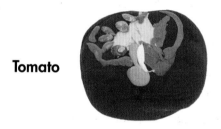

Tomato

1 Make about twelve little balls of purple.

2 Stick them together in a pyramid.

Grapes

1 Make a ball of green and squeeze the top to narrow it.

2 Add a small stalk and some darker streaks near the top.

Pear

1 Make a yellow sausage. Narrow the ends almost into points.

2 Put small pieces of brown on the ends, and add some brown streaks.

Banana

Snail
Spiral Patterns

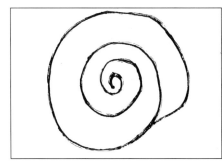

Fig 1

Theme

A Snail
Spirals and patterns

Materials

Paper   white or coloured
Crayons   wax, water soluble
   or oil crayons

Starting Point

Look at a picture of a spiral,
Fig1, or if you have one look at
a snail shell or a spiral seaside
shell. See how the spiral goes
round and round.

Draw some spirals in the air
with your finger or on a spare
piece of paper.

Preparation

Cover the table and lay out
your materials.

Trouble Shooter

It is very important when
drawing the shell to leave
room for the rest of the snail.

Method

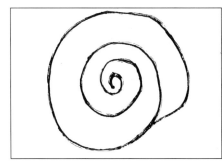

1   In order to get the centre
    point fold your paper twice
    then open it out. Mark the
    centre with a dark crayon.

2   From the centre point start
    drawing a spiral using a
    dark crayon.

3   Stop the spiral about 1/2
    way down one side of the
    shell leaving enough room
    for the snail's head and
    body. Add the head and
    body.

4 Using just one colour, make patterns around the shell and on the snail's head and body.

5 Colour in the patterns using contrasting light and dark colours.

6 Add in any other details and some background if you wish.

Finger Puppets

Suggested Themes

People
Animals
Birds

Starting Point

First decide on the character
of your puppet, whether
it is going to be an animal,
a person or a bird.

Materials

Felt or material

cut into strips of 10 cm
long and the height of
your finger

Glue
Newspaper
Decoration

Feathers
Beads
Wool

Equipment
Scissors

Preparation

Cover the table with newspaper.

1   Roll the felt strip loosely
around your finger and glue
the side to make a tube.

2   Bend the top over itself and
glue it down. The two sides
can be left standing up for
ears if making an animal.

6   Cut out eyes, from black
and white felt, and glue
them in position.

7   Cut the mouth shape
and glue it on.

3 Fold the two sides in and glue if making a person.

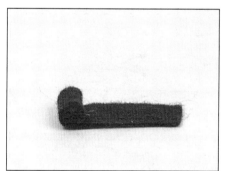

4 Cut a strip for the nose 1cm wide and quite long (the longer you cut it the fatter the nose will be). Roll it up tightly and glue the side.

5 Stick it on to the front of your puppet.

8 Add on hair, moustaches beards etc.

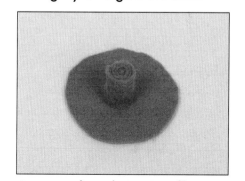

9 To make a hat, cut a long strip and roll it up like the nose. Cut a circle. Glue the rolled up strip in the centre of the circle.

10 Glue the hat on and add any other details you choose.

13

Foldies

1   Fold your sheet of paper in half, then open it out again. You will have a fold mark down the centre.

Theme

The patterns achieved by folding paper when the paint is still wet.

2   Cover your sheet of paper with an even coat of one colour. Paint all your brush strokes first horizontally and then vertically so that the page is completely filled in.

Materials

Paper   white cartridge
Paint   water based

Equipment

Paint brushes
Tubs   for paint and water
Newspaper

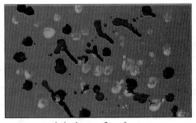

3   Put wet blobs of other chosen colours all over your paper.

Trouble Shooter

Though you must apply the paint for your background and blobs very thickly, if you overdo it, it may crack off later. Remember that you must use larger amounts of lighter colours as the darker colours will swamp the lighter. If you don't remember which are the primary colours look at the activity on page 6.

4   Refold your page. Rub it very gently from the centre fold to the edge.

Preparation

Cover the table with newspaper, also anywhere you might be going to put the paintings to dry. You will need a lot of space. Have hand washing facilities within easy reach, as this activity can be very messy.

Method

It works best to cover the whole sheet of paper with one colour. While it is still damp blob on spots of other colours.
It is essential that these blobs are still wet when the page is folded. Trial and error will show you the amounts to use to achieve the effect you want.

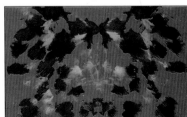

5   Open it out carefully. Leave it to dry.

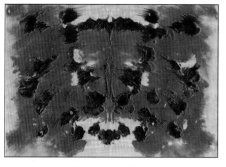 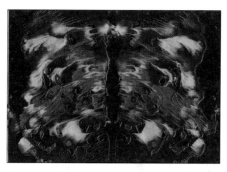 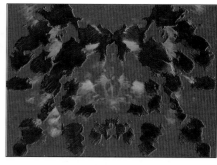

Primary colours achieve interesting effects when they mix to make secondary colours.
Apply one primary colour as a background and spot with the other two.

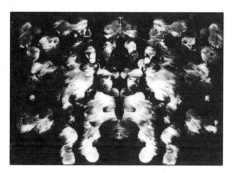 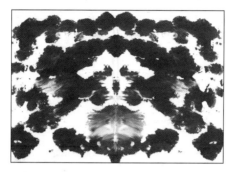 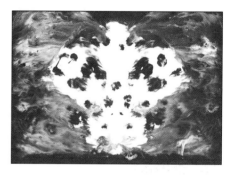

Black and white make ghostly pictures. Use black and spot with white or use white and spot with black.
You could use a black and white background and spot with black and white.

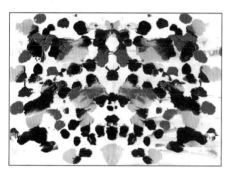 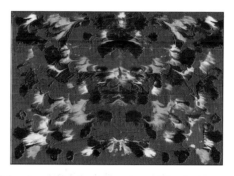 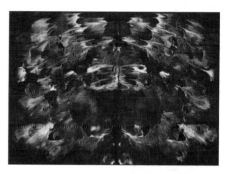

Make some coloured pictures with black and white spots added in.
It is interesting to see how black and white make colours appear brighter and more intense.

 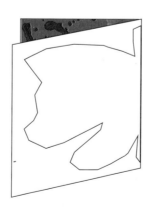 

When your pages are dry, you can use them to make colourful shapes if you wish.
Fold the page over and draw the shape of half a butterfly. Cut out the doubled shape.

Witch Silhouette

Suggested Themes

Witches dancing
The haunted house
Howl at the moon
Fancy dress party
Bonfire night
Bats
The creepy cemetery
Demons
The witch's cat
Pumpkin lanterns
Halloween

Starting Point

Think about Autumn evenings, bonfires and festivals.

Materials

Paper   black sugar
            white cartridge
            newspaper
Paper plates
Paint   red and yellow
            (water based for
            mixing)
Chalk   white
PVA glue

Equipment

Scissors
Kitchen roll (tissue)
Paint brushes
Water containers

Preparation

First cover all tables with newspaper or similar paper. Pour the red and yellow paint on to separate paper plates. Use one brush for red and one for yellow, this helps to stop mixing up the paint too much.

Method

1 Paint the page. Apply the paint smoothly and evenly with horizontal strokes to cover the page. Allow the paint to overlap this will give a dramatic effect and new colours.

When changing colour wash your brush in water and dry it off with tissue. Too much water will ruin the effect. The page can be painted to give the effect of an autumn evening sky, dark colours at the top gradually lightening towards the bottom.

When the whole page is painted leave it to dry.

2 On black sugar paper draw the silhouettes with chalk. Cut them out taking care not to make them too small. Simple clear shapes give the best results.

3 Arrange the silhouettes in position, putting the larger ones to the front and smaller ones to the back. Do not glue anything in place until you are certain everything is in the correct position.

1 Paint the page.

2 Cut out black silhouettes.

3 Glue the silhouettes in position.

Trouble Shooter

Using too much water with the paint ruins the effect.

Don't make the silhouettes too small as they become hard to handle.

Avoid very intricate shapes.

Tissue Fish

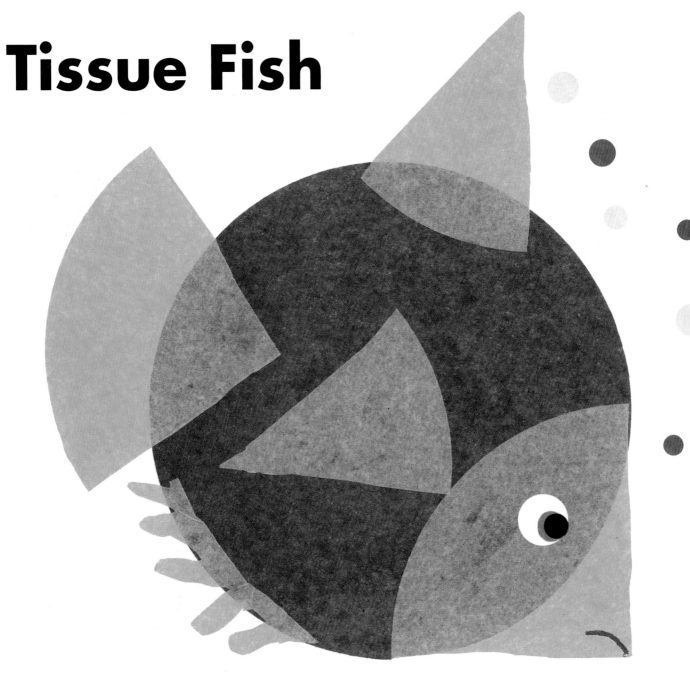

Theme
Colourful fish

Materials
Paper   white
               coloured tissue circles
Glue
Stickers small round
Newspaper

Equipment
Scissors
Pencil
Felt tip pens

Starting Point
Decide on the colours and type of fish you want to make.

Preparation
Cover the tables with newspaper and lay out your materials. Two tissue circles make one fish.

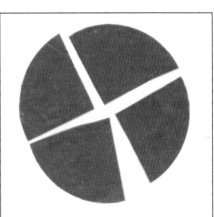

1 Choose what colours you would like your fish to be. Fold one circle in half and then in quarters. Open it out. Cut the circle into quarters.

Trouble Shooter

Tissue paper rips very easily so only glue when you are sure everything is in the correct position, as it is impossible to pull apart.

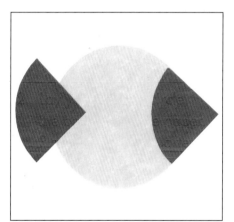

2   Lay your second circle, the body, on white paper. Place one of the quarters in position for the head. Place another in position for the tail.

3   Cut another quarter in half and place the pieces in position for the fins.

4   Glue everything in place. Stick the stickers in position for the eyes and draw in fin lines and scales on to your fish.

Finger Painting

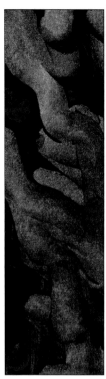

Theme

Choose a dramatic subject that will give lots of scope for free finger painting.
A Bonfire
A Shipwreck
Fireworks
A Volcano
An Autumn Storm

Materials

Finger Paints
Paper   white cartridge
Tissue   to wipe fingers

Starting Point

Spoon some finger paint on to a paper plate. Dip your finger into it. Spread it on the paper and move your fingers about making patterns.
Always wipe your fingers well between colours.
Practice using the finger paints until you feel you are able to use them easily.

Method

Dip your finger in the finger paint and make an outline of the main feature of your picture as in step 1 for the Shipwreck, Bonfire, Fish and Volcano.
With your fingers smear and dab the rest of the picture in until you have covered up every bit of the page.

Equipment
Disposable Spoons
Paper Plates
Newspaper

Preparation

Cover the work surface with newspaper.
Have lots of tissue within easy reach.

Trouble Shooter

Be careful mixing colours with your fingers. If you have several colours on the page and you mix them together too thoroughly you will end up with a muddy brown colour.
Don't put painty fingers covered in one colour into a different colour as you will ruin it.

A Shipwreck

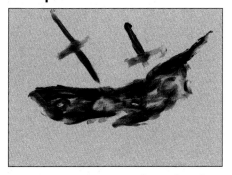 

1 Start with an outline sketch of the shape of the wreck.

2 Put in the stormy sky, rolling the paint around with your fingers.

3 Rub in the wild sea from green, blue and black, with white spots of foam.

A Bonfire

1 With your finger sketch in the sticks in the bonfire.

2 Smear in the flames from yellow, red and a little black.

3 Fill the rest of the picture with smoke, rolling it around with your finger.

A Fish

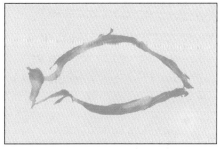  

1 Outline the fish.

2 Fill it in with smears and dabs of different colours.

3 Put in more fish or bubbles and seaweed.

A Volcano

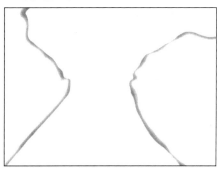 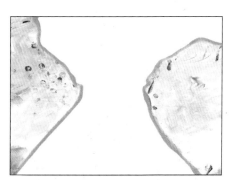 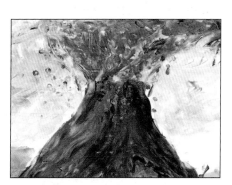

1 Smear in the outline of the volcano.

2 Put in the smoky sky.

3 Fill the rest of the picture with flames and exploding rocks and rivers of lava.

Candles

Theme
Coloured Candles

Materials
Wax   solid or flaked paraffin wax
Wax Dyes   different colours
Moulds   shop moulds or polystyrene cups
Wick
Skewers
Clay or Putty
Mixing cups   paper cups or tins

Preparation
Cut lengths of wick the height of your mould plus 7.5cm extra. If using polystyrene cups, punch a hole in the end so the wick can be threaded through. Melt the wax, mark 1 on the deep fat fryer, to a temperature of 100°c. Soak the wick in the molten wax then take it out and set it aside. Thread the hardened wick through the hole in your mould. Seal the end with clay or putty Fig 1. Place a skewer across the open end of the mould and wrap the wick around it so it stays vertical Fig 2.

Equipment
Knife
Deep fat fryer

Starting Point
Choose the shape and colour you want your candle to be.

Fig 1

Fig 2

Stripy Candles
Method

1. Your first coloured layer is made by chipping a small amount of the dye disc into the bottom of a mixing cup. Pour molten wax in on top of it and stir with a skewer until all of the dye disc has dissolved. The more dye disc you put in the darker the colour will be. Pour it into the mould.

Don't overheat the wax as it may melt the polystyrene cups. Spray shop moulds with lubricating oil spray so that the candle slides out easily.

Do not pull the candle out by the wick.

Make sure you seal the end of the mould well with clay or putty or else the wax will leak out.

Do not get wax on clothes. Dip the finished candle once in the hot melted wax to get a bright shine.

2 A second coloured layer can be added when the wax has cooled down enough so you can press your finger into the surface, denting it, but no molten wax breaks through.

3 Add as many layers as you want and fill up the mould. Leave it to cool down completely.

4 When it is cold, peel off the polystyrene cup. If using a shop mould slide it out.

Hand Prints

Theme

Hand prints made into colourful pictures.
Feathers on a bird
Scales on a fish
Petals on a flower
Hair on animals
Leaves on a tree

Starting Point

Think of hands and what they might look like if you put lots of them together to make a picture.

Materials

Paper   white cartridge
white practice
coloured
newspaper
Paint   coloured
water based
PVA glue
Pencils

Equipment

Paint brushes
Paper plates
Scissors
Hand basin
Soap
Towel

Preparation

Cover the tables with plenty of newspaper. Use a separate plate and brush for each colour paint.

Method

1   Place your practice paper on the table. Choose a colour and paint your hand.

2   Spread your fingers out as wide as you can then carefully print your hand. When you are confident with your prints use your white cartridge paper.

3   Each time you change colour wash your hand and dry it. Print lots of hands and let them dry. Once dry cut them out carefully.

Sun Flower

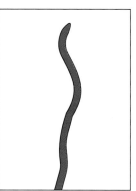

1   On a large piece of paper draw and colour the stem of your Sun Flower.

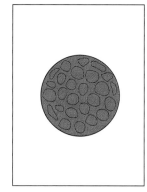

2   Cut a large circle out of coloured paper for the middle of the flower and colour in the seeds.

3   Glue the bottoms of your cut out hand prints around the middle in a circle so the fingers stick up to form the petals.

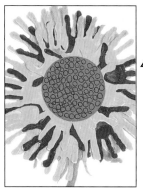

4   Glue at least three rows of hands letting them overlap.

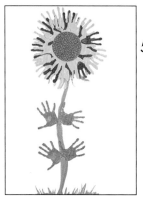

5   Glue your flower onto the top of the stem. Add leaves using green hand prints.

Bird

Method

1 On a large piece of paper draw the outline of a bird.

2 Colour in the beak and the legs.

3 Starting at the tail end of the bird begin to glue your cut out hand prints in position so they stick up to become the feathers.

4 Let the hands overlap and fill the body.

5 Cut out eyes from coloured paper and glue them in position.

Trouble shooting

Spread your hands out as wide as you can when printing to make cutting out easy.
Don't shake, wobble or slip when printing as you will ruin the hand print.

Clocks

Suggested Themes

Clocks
Weather
Time
The Seasons
Different Emotions

Starting Point

Choose what type of clock
you would like to make.

Materials

Paper plates
Coloured card/paper
Glue
Felt tip pens
Paper fasteners

Equipment

Scissors
Rulers
Pencils

Preparation

Cover the tables
with newspaper.

Number clock
Method

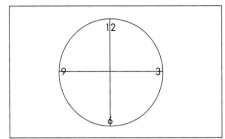

1   Divide the clock into four
    equal parts with a pencil.
    Number each point, 12 at
    the top 6 at the bottom 9 to
    the left and 3 to the right.

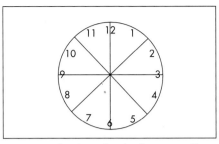

2   Divide the clock diagonally
    twice and add in the other
    numbers in the spaces.

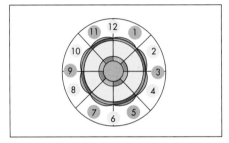

3   Colour in the face of the
    clock. Add extra details
    to the face with coloured
    card or paper.

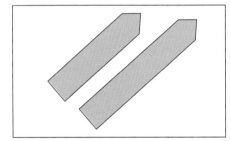

4   Cut out two arms,
    the minute hand and
    the hour hand.

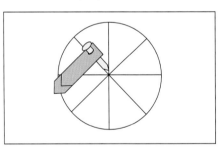

5   Push the paper fastener
    through the end of both
    arms and the centre point
    of the clock.

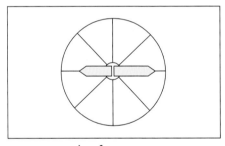

6   Open the fastener out at
    the back of the clock.

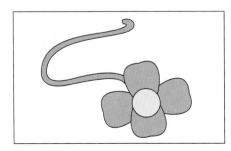

Pendulum

7   Cut a long strip of paper/
    card and glue a circle on
    the end.

8   Glue the pendulum on
    to the clock.

Trouble Shooter

Make a hole through the hands and the centre of the clock before trying to push the paper fastener through.

Emotion clock

1   Divide your plate into 4 equal parts. Think of faces expressing 4 different emotions and draw them into your spaces and colour them in.

2   Cut two arms and attach them with a paper fastener.

3   Add any other details you choose.

Weather Clock

1   Divide your plate into 4 equal parts. Draw a weather type into each space and colour them in.

2   Cut out two arms and attach them with a paper fastener.

3   Add any other details you choose, clouds, lightning bolts etc.

A House and Garden

Preparation

Lay out your tools beside the board and start with a piece of clay about the size of a small melon.

Theme

A House and Garden

Materials

Pottery Clay

or other type of modelling clay

Paints acrylic or powder paint mixed with PVA glue

Equipment

Modelling Tools

or

Tools improvised from skewers and lollypop sticks

Boards hardboard with a textured side is best. It stops the clay sticking when it is pressed down.

Starting Point

Think about the shape of a house and what every house needs, like a roof, door and windows.

Trouble Shooting

As this house is not going to be hardened by the firing process it will depend on the coating of acrylic paint or paint mixed with PVA glue to hold it together. Don't have any long thin bits sticking out or they will break off. If you handle your clay too much it will become overworked and full of cracks. If this happens get a new piece and put your first piece back in a plastic bag, seal it, and it will recover.

Method

1 Form your clay into three balls, one larger than the other two.

5 Use the remaining clay to make a roof.

2 Flatten the larger ball to make a base for your house at least 2 cm thick and roughly rectangular.

3 Take one of the other balls and bang it on the board, first one side then the others to form a cuboid for the main part of the house.

4 Make some rolls from about half of the remaining ball and keep to use for details in the house and garden.

6 Add details like doors, windows, chimneys and plants to the house and garden.

7 When the clay is thoroughly dry, paint the house and garden.

8 Paint lots of detail on the sides of the house and in the garden.

Family Pictures

At the Supermarket with Granny by Laura aged 4

When Laura was painting her picture, first she painted the things she saw at the supermarket — rows of mushrooms, apples and bananas.

Then she put in a big piece of bacon because she likes bacon.

Then she painted her Granny pushing a trolley full of shopping and herself pushing a smaller one.

Last of all she put in the cash register.

Theme

A picture about yourself
A picture about you and your family doing something interesting

Materials

Paints water based
Paper coloured

Equipment

Paint brushes
Tubs for paint and water
Newspaper

Starting Point

Think about what you would like to put into your picture. When you start you will think of other things to add in.

Preparation

Cover the tables and lay out your materials.

Method

Start sketching in your picture with a thin paint brush then use the fat brush to fill in the thick bits. When you have finished write a caption for you picture.

Eva's picture is about her Daddy painting and herself and her baby sister in the garden. Eva is six.

William, aged six, painted the dog he had been petting and his Daddy playing golf.

Fintan, aged 6, painted himself and his Mum and Dad picking vegetables.

Pom Pom Birds

Theme
Birds

Starting Point
Choose the colour of
your bird and what sort
of character it will be.

Materials
Wool
Felt
Card
Pipe Cleaners
Glue

Equipment
Scissors
Compass
Pencils

Preparation
With a compass and pencil
draw a circle 7.5 cm diameter
on to card and cut it out.
In the centre of it draw a 3 cm
diameter circle and cut it out.
You will need two of these.

Method

1   Cut a long length of wool.
Put the two circles together
and tie them through the
centre. Wrap the wool
around the card, clockwise,
each time going through
the centre.

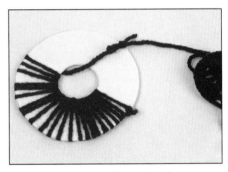

2   When your length of wool
runs out, tie a new piece to
the end of it and continue
wrapping.

6   Tear off the cards and fluff
up the pom pom.

Eyes
7   Cut out circles from paper
or felt for the eyes and glue
them in place.

Trouble Shooter

Tie the wool very tightly around the centre of the pom pom. Do not tear off the card circles until you have tied the centre. When gluing, don't put the glue on the pom pom put it on the added pieces.

3   Wrap until the centre has completely filled up. Tie off the end.

4   Place your scissors between the card circles and cut the wool all the way around it.

5   Open out the two card circles and slide a piece of wool between the cards and tie it as tight as you can.

Beak

8   Cut a diamond shape out of felt or paper and bend it in half. Glue it in position.

Claws/feet

9   Bend a pipe cleaner to form your bird's feet and glue them in position.

Hats

10   Add a little hat and scarf or whatever else you choose.

Crowns

Preparation

Cut long strips of card 4.5cm wide.

Method

1 Measure the strip of card around your head.

Suggested Themes

Flowers
Butterflies
Ships
Shapes

Materials

Card light
Paper coloured
Glue

Equipment

Scissors
Stapler
Staples

Starting Point

Decide on the type of crown you are making.

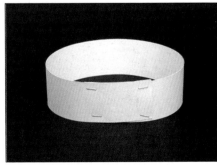

2 Staple the card so it fits comfortably.

Trouble Shooter

Be sure to measure the card around your head before you staple it.

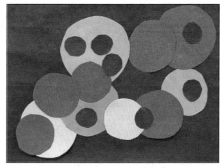

3 Cut out interesting shapes from coloured paper.

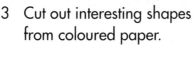

4 Glue them around your crown.

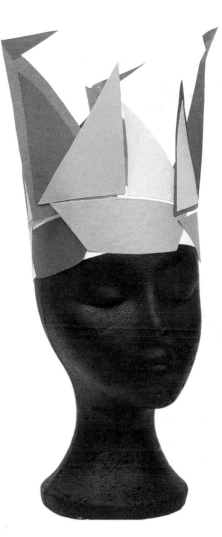

Wax Resist

Suggested Themes

Clowns
People
Kites
Space
Underwater

Materials

Crayons   coloured wax
Paper   white
Paint   water based
               or
Ink   coloured

Equipment

Paint brushes

Starting Point

Decide on the theme of your picture and what colours to use.

Preparation

Cover the tables with newspaper. Mix your paint to a watery consistency.

Method

1   Outline your picture on paper with a light coloured crayon.

Trouble Shooter

Colour the page very heavily with wax crayons.

Mix your paint very watery.

Where you want white you must colour the area with white crayons.

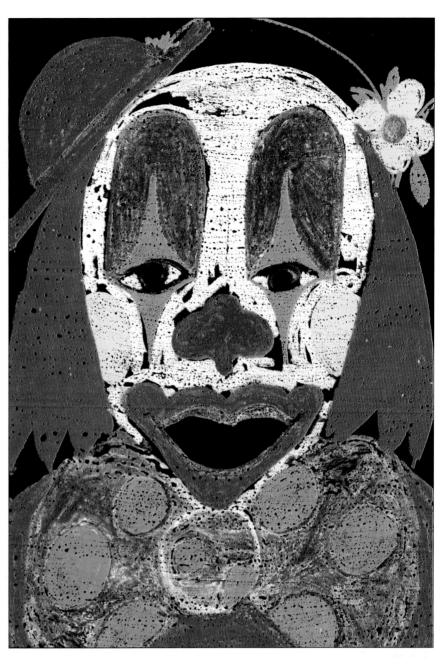

2 Using the crayon very heavily colour in your picture.

3 Paint the entire page with the watery paint or ink.

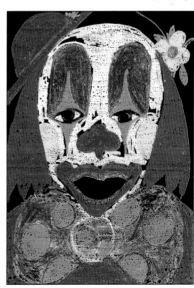

4 Wherever the paint meets the wax it will resist it.

CONE FIGURES

Starting Point
Think of the type of character you would like your person to be.

Preparation
Cover the tables with newspaper and lay out your materials.

Trouble Shooter
Make sure the base of the body sits flat on the table.

Theme
People

Materials
Pipe cleaners
Cotton balls
Card
Paper   newspaper
          coloured

Equipment
Scissors
Stapler
Staples
Glue
Felt tip pens

Method

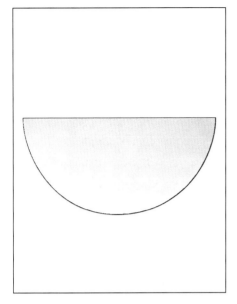

1   Cut your card into a
    half circle.

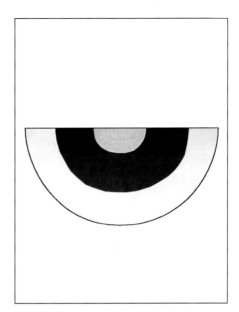

2   Pattern the card to make
    the body of your figure.

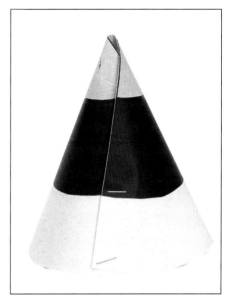

3   Bend the card into a cone
    and staple it to form the body.

4   Pierce two holes in the sides
    of the cone.

5   Thread the pipecleaner
    through the holes to make
    the arms.

6   Draw a face on the cotton
    ball with felt tip pens.
    Glue on hair and any other
    decorations you want,
    then stick your head on top
    of the body.

My Favourite Animal

Theme

A Favourite Animal

Materials

Paint   water based
Paper   white cartridge
           tissue

Equipment

Paint brushes
Tubs   for paint and
         water
Newspaper to cover tables

Preparation

Cover the tables with
newspaper. Lay out the tubs
of paint and water within
easy reach.

Starting Point

Think about the animal you
have chosen to paint.

What is it like ?

Is it fierce or tame ?

Has it got a smooth
or rough coat ?

Has it got big teeth or ears ?

Where does it live ?

What does it eat ?

Method

Your picture is about the
animal, so you must make it
very large. Keep your paint as
dry as possible by wiping as
much of the water off your
brush, with tissues when you
wash it and by wiping the
excess paint off it when you
dip it in the paint tub.

Trouble Shooter

Don't fill in much detail when
you are sketching in the outline
shape, wait until you are
painting in the animal.
Use a paint brush to sketch,
it is very difficult to paint in
a pencil drawing.
If you use the paint too wet the
colours will run into each other.
Use the paint as dry as possible.

1 Sketch in the outline shape of your animal with a thin brush and dark paint.

2 In the background sketch in the place where the animal lives.

3 Sketch what the animal likes to eat.

4 If it fits in with your idea, make a dividing line somewhere on your page to divide the sky from the ground.

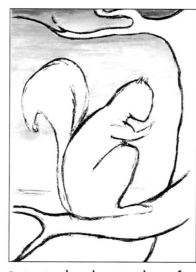

5 Paint in the sky. Use lots of white as well as blue because of all the light there is in the sky.

6 Paint in the background.

7 Paint in the animal's food.

8 Paint in the animal.

9 Paint in any other details.

Teachers' Notes

Rainbows page 6

The **objective** of the activity is to focus on the Spectrum. Mixing Primary colours to make Secondary colours, making colours lighter and darker and changing colours by the addition of other colours are concepts basic to all colour art work. They should be addressed from the earliest years by means of fun projects like painting rainbows. Projects should be **displayed** on the classroom walls for as long as possible. Children absorb a lot from observing their surroundings and if it is their own work it makes it specially relevant. It is very easy to **evaluate** from looking at the children's work whether the child has grasped the concept or not. If not a different project addressing the same art basic in a few weeks' time will probably rectify this.

Things We Eat page 8

Encouraging children to observe shape, form and colour is the **objective** of this activity.
Three dimensional work is a very important part of children's art education. Experimenting with and learning to handle different materials opens the child's mind to the numerous creative possibilities. Modelling helps children develop a sense of proportion and instils habits of observation.
Enumerating and discussing what they have formed and why, is a cross curricular dimension which applies especially to modelling.

Snail Spiral Patterns page 10

This project focuses on pattern. Spirals are one of the basic patterns occurring in nature. Encourage the children to bring in snail shells, sea shells and spiral fossils like ammonites. Get the children to practice drawing spirals on pieces of scrap paper so that they can approach the project with confidence. **Displaying** the snails in a line around the classroom wall enables the children to share each others ideas of pattern. **Evaluate** this activity on manipulative skill in achieving an even spiral, on observation of pattern and on the effect of colour contrast in the designs.

Finger Puppets page 12

As well as developing cutting and sticking skills, the **objective** of this activity is to stimulate the imagination with a fun project. Puppets develop co-operative skills, they can also slot into other areas of the curriculum such as language with little puppet plays worked out by groups of children.

Foldies page 14

This activity focuses on pure colour. It introduces the children to a new and exciting way of applying paint. It draws their attention to the effect colours have on each other and the effect black and white have on colours. Because of its random nature, this activity is a valuable confidence builder, so even less able children can produce startlingly beautiful results. If you are **displaying** a block of Foldies balance the ones with light backgrounds against those with dark. Mount the block on a colour that will bring out the vibrant and dramatic quality of the paint work. Often a white paper background is the most effective. Another way of **displaying** Foldies is a co-operative picture of butterflies or birds or whatever the colours suggest to the children, each child contributing a shape cut from their Foldie.

Witch Silhouette page 16

The **objective** of this activity is to focus on the dramatic quality of a black silhouette on a coloured background. The importance of composing the picture and balancing shape is also addressed. It is easy to **evaluate** the children's awareness of contrast from this activity. This project lends itself to a seasonal display.

Fish page 18

Shape is the focus of this activity, specifically circles of tissue paper and their divisions. The **objective** is to arrange these to form a pleasing and balanced composition. It is a simple way to introduce a very complex concept. These fish display equally well arranged on a window attached by a tiny bit of tape or blue tack or on a white background. The translucent nature of tissue paper expands children's experience of aspects of coloured art work. When **evaluating** the children's grasp of colour balance and shape, remember that tissue paper is quite difficult to handle and is a measure of manipulative skills.

Finger Painting page 20

Finger painting is a very direct way for the children to relate to colour and to paint application. Once they have had some practice and have got used to the feel of paint they ought to be able to apply themselves to this technique in a very uninhibited way. This in turn reflects in the way they subsequently apply paint with a paint brush.

Candles page 22

The **objective** of this activity is to widen the children's experience of creative materials and techniques by introducing them to wax casting. Their satisfaction in creating a beautiful object is greatly increased by having made what they consider an acceptable present to bring home. The element of a successful outcome is very important in fostering a lifelong interest, and confidence in attempting two and three dimensional creative projects.

Hand Printing page 24

Hand printing is often a young child's first introduction to printing. Later they will build on this experience by making repeat prints with a variety of objects. Contributing cut out handprints to a co-operative project gives the owner a part in the eventual outcome and increases interest and involvement.

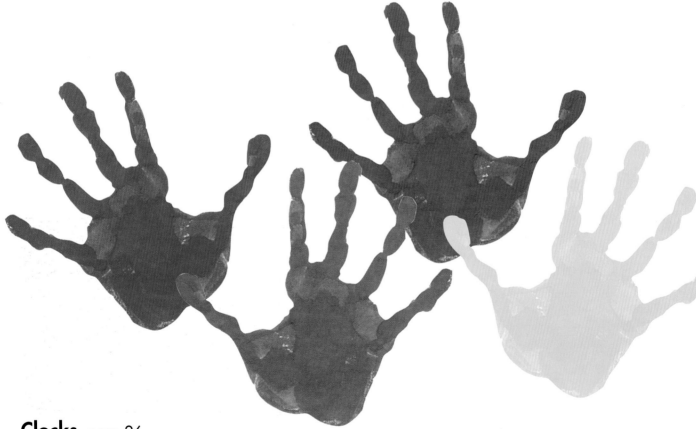

Clocks page 26

This project focuses on the idea of organising the approach to a project before starting. The children become aware that it is necessary to measure and allocate spaces in this type of design. The successful outcome is interesting to the children and can be utilised by them to indicate what the weather is like, what time it is, or how they are feeling.

Houses and Gardens page 28

This project addresses three dimensional form. The **objective** is for the children to succeed in making a small model that they are satisfied with. Once they have achieved the basic house shape, they can then advance to other forms. A small garden gives scope for originality and imagination. **Evaluating** the competence with which the child forms the material is, as with most art work, very obvious from the result.

Family Pictures page 30

This project is approached in a very direct way. Its **objective** is to facilitate the children to express without inhibition how they feel about some family activity. Children under the age of seven are rarely worried by the absence of proportion or perspective from their pictures. They shouldn't be forced to address them at this stage of their development, neither should they be prevented from trying if they wish to. Before starting this activity the children should have had quite a bit of experience with paint. This leaves them free to develop vibrant and balanced compositions. It is an important aspect of this sort of painting that the children should have an opportunity to communicate what the picture is about. This can be done by discussing the content with them and writing a caption. What seems most important to them looms largest. Note the dog in William's painting and the hands in Finbar's. Daddy is very important to Eva who shows her budding sense of proportion in the relative sizes of adult, child and baby.

Pom Pom Birds page 32

This activity **aims** to stimulate the children's imagination and widen their experience of materials and techniques. Yarn can be used in a variety of projects. Making Pom Poms is a very satisfactory technique for young children. There is great scope for creativity in deciding what character to give their Pom Pom.

Crowns page 34

Personal adornment is a very basic application of creativity. The fact that children can wear their creation gives them an added interest in the project. The **objective** is to stimulate innovation and originality, putting together shapes and colours in a personal expression of design.

Clown's Face page 36

The **objective** of this lesson is to give the children a chance to try the technique of wax resist. They learn that if part of their picture is covered in wax it will resist water based paint and ink. The resulting picture has a unique quality. These pictures **display** well on a white background.

Cone Figures page 38

This activity is within the capacity of quite small children. It gives them the opportunity to make a simple standing three dimensional figure. These basic figures can be adapted to become Christmas Angels or Halloween Witches or whatever the child wishes. Once the basic concept has been understood a group project can be initiated, adapting the basic figure.

My Favourite Animal page 40

This project focuses on composition. The step by step nature of the instructions are designed to achieve a satisfactory result while concentrating on the organisation of the foreground and background.
It is important to stimulate the children's interest in their chosen animals by discussion as to where it would live and what it would eat.

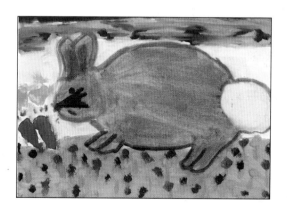